THE GIFT TWICE GIVEN

YVES-MARIE GALETTE

THE GIFT TWICE GIVEN

Authored by Yves-Marie Galette

Copyright©2018

ISBN:9781790826469

Book Cover Copyright©2018

All Scripture References are taken from the King James Version of The Holy Bible

DEDICATION

To my Lord and Savior Jesus Christ, whose perfect love for me has revolutionized my life, banished all my fears and has caused me to walk always in victory. Lord, thank you from the bottom of my heart. You have become my One, Magnificent Obsession.

ACKNOWLEDGMENTS

To my children Gregory, Ashley, and Randy for believing in me.

God, keep making me a better mom just for you.

Sincere thanks to Roger and Margarette Denis, Natalie St. Eloi and all those who helped me, prayed for me, and provided wise counsel during such a critical season in my life.

Thank you also goes to all the destiny helpers whom God strategically placed on my path to inspire me to not give up.

TABLE OF CONTENTS

ENDORSEMENTS

I have had the awesome privilege of knowing Yves-Marie for many years but never knew "her compelling story". What a compelling story of God's redeeming love as she walks us through her faith journey. Yves-Marie has a relentless passion to see people walk in the abundance of God's love. I believe her life story will impact women who made the decision to terminate their pregnancy to receive forgiveness but also prayerfully will be a deterrent to those who feel they have no other option. May they see that even as God provided and protected Yves-Marie and her children; He will do the same for each of us.

Linda Vega
CEO-First Capital Solutions Inc.

The Gift Twice Given is an awesome testimony of God's "unfailing love, abounding grace, and new mercies" toward anyone who will believe in Him. This book is a must-read for anyone faced with crisis and life choices that oppose your faith and moral integrity. With child-like faith, prayer, and a believing heart in God, you can have a breakthrough miracle to overcoming victory and joy.

God's love and mercy are gifts, free to all who will ask and believe!"

Dr. Belinda Campbell
World In Prayer International

Yves-Marie's memoir, *The Gift Twice Given*, will encourage many women who deal with shame and regrets to open their hearts to a loving savior who will love them beyond their greatest darkness and deepest pain. We often believe that in the midst of seemingly dark and lonely moments, God isn't there. We can also mistakenly believe that our darkness and sins repel us from God's love and forgiveness. Yves-Marie's experiences during this insurmountable time is a reminder that the light of God's love can penetrate the darkest of darkness and God can use these difficult times to give us opportunities to explore our inner lives in the light of His presence. As you read Yves-Marie's memoir about the gift of life, allow its message of hope, redemption, and restoration to cause you to bask in the everlasting love of a Heavenly Father who doesn't stand ready to judge and condemn but who stands ever ready as a Righteous Judge to show grace and mercy. His mercy triumphs over judgment (James 2:13)

Your sister in Christ,

Acacia Slaton, Author of "*The Serpent Beguiled Eve*."

This is a touchy story of Yves-Marie's journey through not only a dreaded decision but also the pain and consequences of the decision. But God...the story will show you the love the Father has for you even when you sin and His desire to restore and guide you to a good and satisfying life. He is the God of second chances.

Chantie Holland, Founder, and Revivalist of Foundations Ministries

FOREWORD

I remember first meeting Yves Marie when she walked into Renaissance one Sunday morning. I knew right away she had a life message to share which would help set many people free to live a victorious life. As I began to observe the room, I noticed that she worshipped Jesus without any inhibition, in total freedom. Her passion is contagious, and her story is healing.

In this book, Yves Marie generously writes her odyssey with humor coupled with authenticity and vulnerability that releases life to the human soul. So many people, including myself, grew up with the wrong perspective and understanding of who God is. I viewed God has a harsh, angry, judgmental God that punishes and brings wrath to humanity. This caused me to live a life of hopeless victim. I had the wrong perception of God. The truth is, God is Love, and He loves you more than you know. This book depicts the love of God in the midst of difficulty and life challenges.

Through it all, we must remember that the purpose of challenges and struggles in the valley or wilderness reveals the nature of God, Who He is. I call it the "Face of God," The face of God in every circumstance. In the journey shared in this book, you will see the face of God revealed as the God of Grace, God of Mercy, the God who is faithful to His promises, the God of the Turnaround, and the God who is Always Good.

My hope for you is that you experience God in such a tangible way in your present-day challenges. Romans 8:28 says, "And we know that God causes all things to work together for good to those who love God, to those who are called according to *His* purpose. (NASB95)." If your situation or circumstance is not good, God is not done.

May wholeness be your portion as God secures you in His love and advances you with great hope. His promises are "yes" and amen. God is not a man that He should lie. I pray that you will find God in every moment, every challenge, and every circumstance knowing that He is for you, not against you. This is Yves Marie's story, but it's your life!

Tony Kim

Founder and Co-Senior Leader of Renaissance International; Founder of Roar Collective & Roar Academy; US National Director of Harvest International Ministry (HIM)

INTRODUCTION

The Lord put in my heart to write this book at The Call DC while fasting and praying with Lou Engle and several well-known Church leaders and a multitude of other believers on the Mall in Washington. It was there that I heard women of all ages, races, and walks of life candidly share about their anguish and the pain and torment they suffered after having abortions. I cried the entire time and thanked the Lord for what He had done for me.

As I was intently listening to the testimonies, The Lord spoke quietly to me, "Share your story and tell them about women like you who are faced with this decision."

I have been trying rather unsuccessfully for the past ten years to write this book. However, I finally understand that God in His divine wisdom held me back from sharing my story prematurely. The book would not have reflected who He really is - an Awesome God, a good Father, whose love for His children reaches higher than the highest heaven.

For most of my life, all I heard was that God will judge you if you sin, that you will lose your salvation. I saw Him like my natural father - waiting to crush me for the slightest mistake. I never saw Him as a Father who loves His children.

I did not know anything at all about God's grace or His mercy. Even after the events that I will recount in this book transpired, I still did not know that God loves me. I was an orphan both in the natural and in the spiritual realm.

For the past ten years, I have been trained in the School of the Holy Spirit, whereby The Holy Spirit Himself has been revealing to me God's grace and His mercy through the person of Jesus Christ. Through a personal encounter with the Holy Spirit, I experienced the love of the Father for me. It is through this fresh revelation of God's unfailing love, abounding grace and new mercies that I will discuss my encounter with the grace and mercy of God through Jesus Christ some twenty-four years ago.

I had no idea until July 4, 2018, whom my audience was to be. A friend to whom I had forwarded the manuscript to, asked me: "Who are you writing to?" My answer was immediate, "the Church." I then realized that The Holy Spirit was redirecting me. He went on to tell me that the Church was having abortions in the spirit just as in the natural, especially in the Black Church. Some abort for economic reasons. Some because of their careers but the majority of abortions is because of the sins of premarital sex or fornication.

Very few churches are preaching the message of purity. Holiness is only in appearance or judged by the way one dresses but not by the way one lives. Hyper-grace has ushered in a tolerance to sin that is contrary to the written word of God. It seems as if everything goes. "God is love. Everything will be fine."

Really?

This book is the prequel to my next two books "The Pursuit of Holiness," which addresses the subject of holiness and purity, and "Spiritual Consequences of Abortion," which deals with the rights the enemy now has to harass you if you don't repent and plead the blood of Jesus over the sin.

Yves-Marie Galette

CHAPTER 1

DISCOVERY TO DECISION

Behold, children are a gift of The Lord. The fruit of the womb is a reward. (Psalms 127:3)

In April 1994, I was working the night shift as a Licensed Practical Nurse at a facility for the elderly in New York while attending nursing school during the day to become a Registered Nurse. I had a set routine where I gave the residents their medications, changed their dressings and then sat at the desk for several hours to chart their progress. One night, one of the residents who suffered from Alzheimer's got out of bed and made her way to the nursing station undetected. She suddenly pulled the chair that I was about to sit in right from under me. I fell and hit the floor extremely hard and twisted my left knee in the process.

I was rushed to the nearest Emergency Room via ambulance. As expected, because I was a woman of childbearing age, they did a pregnancy test before conducting any X-ray, and to my complete surprise, my test came back positive. This made it impossible for the doctor to X-ray my knee or prescribe anything for the pain in the interest of not wanting to harm the baby.

So, the doctor put my knee back in place; wrapped it with an ace bandage and gave me a pair of crutches with the strict instruction to not put any weight on it for six weeks. I was discharged from the hospital at 4 AM. I opted not to call my husband and wake up the children who had to be in school at eight. I took a cab to the World Trade Center, and then took the train to New Jersey and another cab to my house when I got to Newark Penn Station.

I was very apprehensive going home because I not only had to tell my husband that I was pregnant with our third child but also tell him that there would not be any paychecks for the next six weeks because I would not be able to work. I had been employed at that facility for less than a year, so disability insurance would not kick in. I expected some reluctance, even some degree of complaining, but not the vicious fight that followed.

I was accused of using children as a means to keep our family poor. I could have reminded him that we were in financial trouble because of him. He quit his salaried position in support of a co-worker who got fired for stealing. Where was the concern for our family and our financial wellbeing then? Our marriage was already on shaky ground. However, this pregnancy was the last straw. My husband ended his verbal tirade with a resounding: "We can't have this baby. Take care of it."

The days that followed were tense. We exchanged angry glares in the presence of our children Gregory and Ashley but no words. I made an appointment with Dr. K., my gynecologist. Dr. K. confirmed that I was eight weeks pregnant via sonogram with a due date of December 10. My hope of getting support from my mother and my closest friends was quickly dashed when everyone sided with my husband Victor. Part of it I believe is our culture, as the Haitian man is the head of the house. Whatever he says is law. The other part was that all of them were unbelievers in Jesus. They did not see anything wrong with removing "a blot clot" as they put it. They told me that my primary concern should be for my two living children, not the unborn one. I found no sympathy in them.

The nagging was constant. I was told that life was not a fairy tale; that it was time to grow up.

Alas, the majority won. Looking back over this season of my life, I can see why I caved under the pressure. I did not know the promises of God for myself. I had not memorized any scriptures. I went to church and did religion but really did not know God.

This one particular scripture drew me every time I looked at it. It was everywhere on Christian television: "But seek first his kingdom and his righteousness, and all these things will be given to you as well," Matthew 6:33. I had no idea what it meant to "seek the Kingdom." I knew with a certainty, however, that having an abortion was not a righteous act. I had compromised my values. I took the path of least resistance.

In my ninth week of pregnancy, I made an appointment to terminate it. My appointment was on a Wednesday. A friend dropped me off at the surgical center where my obstetrician was to perform a dilation and curettage procedure under general anesthesia.

The second I got out of the car a wave of nausea hit me so strongly that I doubled over. My friend said in a very matter-of-fact tone, "It will all be gone when I pick you up this afternoon." I made no response as I slowly walked through the entrance, dejected and defeated, on my way to carry out a death sentence on my unborn baby. The Bible tells us: "God abhors hands that shed innocent blood." (Proverbs 6:17) Who is more innocent than an unborn baby in the safety of a mother's womb?

As I looked around, I remembered that I had vowed never to do the very thing I was about to do. I made this vow as a teenager after a male relative who had molested me took me to a private clinic to hide the evidence of his wrongdoing. All I remember from the incident is being introduced as his daughter who was in trouble. I was given two pills to drink and waited in a sitting area fully clothed. I woke up about three hours later, groggy but fully clothed, with no evidence that a painful procedure had been performed on my person. I had vowed to myself that I would never even consider abortion as an option in my life, that once I became an adult no one would ever force me to do anything against my will.

Yet, here I was, a married woman with two children about to eat my very words. That reality did not go down easily. I was desperately looking for a way out but there seemed to be no way out for my baby.

I reluctantly followed the nurse, who came to fetch me from the waiting area into a procedure room where I changed into a gown and got onto a gurney. She then inserted an intravenous line into my left arm and started fluid running. She then wheeled me to the operating room where the procedure would be performed. The nurse anesthetist was busy preparing medications.

The doctor was not yet in the room, so with what little time I had to myself I said quietly, "Lord I wish there was another way. I don't want to do this. I want my baby." I did not think of these simple words as a prayer, I was too ashamed to even think about praying to God. I felt more like the tax collector in the temple beating his chest confessing that he was a sinner, unworthy to look up to heaven. I thought that I deserved the fires of hell since I was guilty of murder.

Finally, both the doctor and nurse anesthetist approached me and spoke something to me that I cannot recall. The only thing I do remember is counting backward from ten to seven. I woke up an hour later in the recovery room, the intravenous line had been removed and a band-aid covered the site. The nurse, seeing that I was awake, came over handed me some Motrin and a cup of juice, which I refused. I felt no right at all to alleviate my pain after the terrible sin I just committed.

An hour later, after consuming some mandatory juice and crackers, the nurse performed one last check to ensure that I was not bleeding heavily; I was discharged with instructions to follow up in six weeks with my doctor and to call if I had experienced severe pain or excessive bleeding. My friend had been notified by the front desk that I was in recovery was already waiting for me outside.

I left the place hunched over, miserable and totally enveloped in a black cloud that weighed me down heavily.

I kept hearing over and over in my head "murderer" like some kind of demonic chant. When I finally made it to my friend's car I pretended that I was in too much pain to talk. Upon observing my countenance, she decided not to say anything else.

Thank God! We spent the duration of the ride to my home in total silence. I wanted to go to my room and hide from the world, but how could I hide from myself or God?

Something died in my heart that day. I said goodbye to my girlish dream of finding a knight in shining armor, a life companion who would protect me, support me and provide for our children - you know, a man unafraid of hard work or sacrifices for his family - a good man. That day, I vowed never to depend on anyone again.

CHAPTER 2

MY WOUNDED SOUL

I heard "Murderer!" being whispered into my ears day and night by the accuser Satan, although I did not know it was him at the time.

The next six weeks were awful. I walked around depressed and weighted down by guilt, shame, and condemnation. I did not enjoy time alone with my children. In fact, I would only touch them when it was absolutely necessary. I felt that the less contact with them, the better, for fear of contaminating them.

I felt so dirty. How could I love them when I had just murdered their sibling, and thrown God's gift back into His face? I felt so alone.

I went to school every day hopping on my crutches and smiling and interacting with different people while being in complete and utter turmoil inside. There was no one to confide in. I did not pray, believing that God had turned His back completely on me and that I was no longer saved.

That was the worst part. My relationship with my mom was on the cool side, so we did not talk as often as we used to, and when we did talk it was just about mundane stuff, definitely not the heart-to-heart we usually have. I isolated myself from my friends because they had abortions and thought I was making a big deal out of nothing. I was so angry with my husband! I could not even look at him without wanting to throw something at him. I kept thinking, all you had to do was work a second job for six months until I graduated from nursing school. Would that have killed you?

"No, it wouldn't have," I thought to myself, "but the selfish man, made me commit murder instead." I knew that it was only a matter of time before we went our separate ways. The marriage that was already struggling was now crumbling faster than I thought possible.

I could not get over the baby, so, to fuel my anger and to fulfill my vow to be fully independent, I immersed myself in my studies. I did everything at home like a robot. And like a robot I did not talk much or play with my children, unaware that they were watching my every move. I made the long commute every day from New Jersey to Manhattan with my crutches, catching buses and trains to and from school. My knee did not get any better. I never really rested it as the doctor ordered.

The only thing that kept me going was my drive to graduate from the program. So, I studied. I listened to tapes of the lectures during my commute and I did very well.

I found all kind of excuses to not go to church. I did not pray or read my Bible. I thought, "What's the point? God is not going to listen to me, a sinner, heading straight to hell. He has far more important things to do and children worthier of His time and compassion than me." But as it was, one evening after putting my children to bed, I walked out and closing the door behind me as they asked, I overhead them pray "Jesus please make mommy better she cries all the time and she doesn't play with us. Grandma said she's just not feeling good and we need to be quiet. Can you please give us our old Mommy back? Amen". I stood behind the door unable to move, with bitter tears soaking the front of my nightgown.

I prayed for the first time that night since the abortion. I fell on my bed and just cried and told God how sorry I was and asked Him to please forgive me. I needed to understand how I got to the dark place where I found myself. How could this happen to me? I had been a born-again believer since I was eighteen years old. I married my second boyfriend at twenty-one. Here I was at twenty-seven. I broke the one vow I made to myself, a wow that I had renewed just eighteen months before.

You see, for a little over a year and a half I worked at a big New York City hospital where second-trimester abortions were performed. I was hired in the Maternal Child department and rotated through four different units: Obstetrics; Post-partum; the Nursery and Gynecology on an as-needed basis with my base unit being Gynecology.

The second-trimester abortions were performed on Thursdays. Because I was a float I was rarely there but was trained to care for the women under the supervision of a Registered Nurse. The women would come in the morning would be given medications to induce labor and pain medication. They would go through labor and actually give birth to the baby. It was a long, painful and messy process because the side effects of these medications were vomiting and diarrhea. It could take a couple of hours or several hours lasting well into the night.

When I first started the job, I thought that it would be a one-off for the women who came in. I asked myself, "Who in their right minds would want a repeat of this ordeal?" But as time went on I found out that some of these women came as many as three times a year.

I stood on my righteousness and I did what Jesus told us not to do; I judged them. That's when I renewed my vow that I would never consider abortion as a solution.

I left that job after months of having a recurring nightmare in which I got on a city bus to Manhattan, and only I and the driver looked human. All the passengers were fetuses pointing at me chanting in high pitch voices "Murderer, murderer you are a murderer." My last day on the job, two women aborted twins. I could not wait to leave and never look back. Here I was in these women's shoes and I could not handle it. I thought that I was morally upright and better than these women. It turned out that I was not.

I had to face the fact that as a born-again believer, I was a fake, a hypocrite who did not take a stand for God but bowed down to worldly pressure and knowingly made the wrong choice. Even though I did not have a second-trimester abortion, the end result was the same. I killed my baby too.

I longed to play with my children, to hug them and to kiss them and tickle them until they cried for mercy, but I couldn't. I felt that they somehow knew what I did. I started wondering whether the baby I aborted would have looked like them. Would he or she have been as sweet as they were as babies? With so many questions and so many "ifs," would life ever be normal again? How was I going to survive this nightmare?

Yves-Marie Galette

CHAPTER 3

GRACE, MERCY AND THE MIRACLE

The six dreadful weeks had passed and the day finally came for my check up with my obstetrician. I arrived at the doctor's office, signed in and waited to be called. An hour later wrapped tightly in my paper gown, I sat on the exam table after having rung the bell for the nurse to collect the urine specimen that she had requested from me.

First, I waited for thirty minutes. Then the wait turned into forty-five minutes and still no doctor. I was about to open the door and see what was going on when he walked through the door. Dr. K. usually was a happy, jovial man always telling corny jokes but not that day.

He looked very formal and very proper. I got really scared really fast when I saw the nurse bringing the ultrasound machine and other equipment in the room. He finally spoke and said, "Did you have a period in the past six weeks?" I said, "No." Then he said, "I need to do an ultrasound to see what's going on."

I lay down on the exam table. My heart was beating so fast that I started feeling lightheaded. He did the sonogram in silence looking intently at the screen for about twenty minutes. Then Dr. K. wiped the gel off my belly, told me to get dressed and to meet him in his office.

Horrible thoughts raced into my mind at that moment as cold sweat poured down my back. I thought that they might have left a surgical instrument behind, part of the baby or perhaps he saw some huge, cancerous tumor.

What could be so wrong I wondered?

I got dressed with shaky hands and sweaty palms. I had a knot in my throat and my heart was beating like a bird wanting to escape its cage. I was nauseous and dizzy and all of a sudden, I just wanted to play ostrich and bury my head in the sand as to avoid the ominous news. At the very least, I wanted to cover my ears so that I would not hear what he had to say. Childish I know, but that's what I wanted to do!

As providence would have it, the nurse came to escort me to the doctor's office. Dr. K. motioned for me to take a seat as he read my chart. He finally blurted out, "We are going to have to redo the procedure. You are still pregnant." I said, "What?" He repeated, "You are still pregnant. I can take you back tomorrow. Is that ok with you?"

I was crying and saying over and over, "Thank You, Jesus! Oh, thank You, Lord! Thank You, I won't let you down!" I was crying, and shaking uncontrollably. I was in my own world unaware of anything else but the fact that God had given me a second chance. My baby was alive! What a miracle! Thank You, Jesus! Glory to Your name!

The doctor's voice finally penetrated my happiness, "I am assuming you don't need another appointment? You're keeping the baby?" My "Yes!" resounded like rolling thunder in that little room. I proceeded to tell him that I was in Nursing school and that I was not working and had no insurance. He told me, "Don't worry, we will work something out for you."

He wrote me a referral for emergency Medicaid, a prescription for prenatal vitamins, gave me some free samples and sent me to the front desk to make another appointment to see him in two weeks.

I practically danced out of that building. I had now graduated to a cane and was still supposed to put most of my weight on my right leg. I was bubbling with excitement. An excitement that I had not experienced for months. I had to dance. I was smiling and waving at everybody who passed by me.

From the time I left the office, all of my symptoms had vanished.

I was beyond happy. I could not wait to pick up my children from school that day. So, I decided to throw them a party. I stopped at the grocery store for ice cream and ingredients to bake a cake and cooked their favorite dish - lasagna. I bought a Power Ranger toy for my son Greg and a new outfit for my daughter Ashley's Cabbage Patch doll. The kids and I were going to celebrate!

I needed to make amends for my coldness and rejection of the past weeks and really show them how much I loved them. I prepared everything, decorated the table and went to their school, which was only a fifteen-minute ride on the bus.

I suddenly realized that it had been a whole hour since I last thanked Jesus for my miracle. So, I thanked Him over and over. I could not stop smiling.

When I got to their school, I hugged and kissed my children until they begged me to stop. The children were delighted. They screamed on top of their voices, "She's back, she's back!"

We had a feast and played lots of silly games that evening. I apologized and told them that I went to the doctor and everything was fine. After they opened their presents they kissed me and it was my turn to beg for mercy. That night I prayed, repented again for not trusting God and thanked and praised Him for the second chance He gave me. I fell asleep with tears of joy running down my face.

My last thought was that I needed to do some serious plotting and planning if I wanted to keep the pregnancy a secret from everyone until it was too late for an abortion. I had met Grace and Mercy that day in the person of Jesus Christ, although it would be years before I realized it.

CHAPTER 4

SECRET AGENT MOM

I was now in my second trimester. My plan was to keep the pregnancy between myself and my doctor. I started wearing layers and complain all the time that I was cold. I told everyone how stressful school was and how much junk food I ate while studying to explain my weight gain.

Since I was not being intimate with my husband and he had just accepted a night shift position at his job, all I had to do was not undress around him. The challenging part was to not touch my belly and smile; resist the urge to rub my back and keep my food cravings under control. Some days I performed so well that I believe I deserve an Oscar nomination.

I had no classes on Fridays so I scheduled my appointment with Social Services and brought with me the doctor's referral for emergency Medicaid. I got denied at first for making too much money the year before. The caseworker dug deep into my private life. I wanted to protest but I said nothing. I put up with the shame and humiliation because I wanted my baby.

It was a very unpleasant experience, one I know I could never share with my Mom. But God sent help in the person of Melissa, an advocate who worked with me and showed them that I was unable to work, but attending a nursing program that I was about to graduate from in less than five months. They gave me Medicaid for me and my children. I knew the minute I had the baby whether my knee was in good shape or not that I would be going back to work. Meanwhile, I breathed a sigh of relief that the children and I had health insurance.

Adding extra weight on my left knee caused so much pain that it would give out while I was crossing the street or getting on the bus and people would have to help me. I started seeing my obstetrician every week because of elevated blood pressure. I just could not tell anybody what was going on. I kept everything to myself and confided only in God.

I talked to the baby constantly when I was alone. I wanted the baby to know that he or she was welcomed, loved and wanted.

As the pregnancy progressed, I had several tests, including an alpha fetal protein, which determines the presence of birth defects. I did not think twice about it. I knew my baby would be just fine. After all, the God of the universe protected my baby from all manner of instruments coming to destroy him, saving him from sure death. Therefore, He would continue to take care of him. I thank God for this blind faith during that time, because there was no room for doubt and unbelief to enter. All I knew was that I had a big God, who is able to do the impossible.

The following Monday, when I got home from class and picking up the children from aftercare, I had three urgent messages from the doctor's office. Since it was too late to call them, I decided to stop by on my way to school, since my first class was not until eleven that morning. By the time I went to bed that night, I was so exhausted that I went to sleep as soon as my head hit my mountain of pillows. I dreamed, boy did I dream! It was more a nightmare in which I was back at the surgical center and the staff was forcibly restraining me against my will in order to perform an abortion on me. In the dream, I fought. I screamed to no avail then finally I said, "God you gave me a second chance. Don't let them do this! Help me keep my baby." I woke up with tears streaming down my face. My pillow was soaked. I was so upset, but I thanked God for the second chance and made a solemn promise to my unborn child that I would die first before letting anything or anyone hurt him. At some point I knew it was a boy, I just knew. I went back to sleep. This time I felt a sense of peace and security as though someone was watching over me ready to intervene at the slightest sign of danger. I did not wake up again until seven that morning when the alarm went off.

CHAPTER 5

LIAR, LIAR PANTS ON FIRE

I dropped Greg and Ashley off at school at 8:30 AM and arrived promptly at Dr. K.'s office at 9 AM. I was the third patient on the sign-in list. I was only in the waiting area ten minutes when the doctor himself came to get me. He told the other two women waiting that I was only there for a test result, and motioned for me to follow him.

I sat on the chair that he held for me and

he walked around to his desk, sat down and opened my chart. I finally noticed that he was not his usual cheerful self. He, in fact, looked very serious. Dr. K. put his pen down looked straight at me and said "There is no other way to say this; your baby more than likely has Down Syndrome. The test you took last week came back very low which is indicative of that kind of birth defect. We have a very small window for an abortion you have no later than a week from today to make a decision."

I enunciated every word very slowly and carefully, "I do not want an abortion." Dr. K. got my message loud and clear. He went on to say: "Knowing you, I anticipated your refusal. I scheduled you tomorrow at the hospital for an amniocentesis. They will insert a needle in your belly, go where the baby is and remove some fluid so we can do chromosomal studies to know for sure where we stand." He continued, "You still have to have the amniocentesis because children with Down Syndrome can also have serious heart defects that require NICU (neonatal intensive care unit) specialists to be present during delivery." Dr. K. then went over the test and what to expect, gave me the referral and a written order for the hospital Obstetrics Department.

I left the office with an arm full of pamphlets to read, wanting so desperately to speak to my mom or even one of my friends, just to talk. But God in His wisdom did not let this happen. They would have pumped me full of doubt and unbelief and caused me to miss my promise. As I sat on the Express Bus to New York City, I kept saying to myself "No, no, and no! There is nothing wrong with my baby! God would not miraculously save his life only to turn his back on him now." Even though I was a baby Christian, God graced me with the faith to believe Him and not what science was saying. So, every time Down Syndrome came to my mind, I just said "No!"

As the day went by I realized that I was not scared, I felt at peace. My only concern was how big that needle was going to be to go through my belly, uterus and amniotic sac. I began talking to the baby like he could understand. Everything I could not tell other people I told him. I even told him to look just like me.

Years later, I would find out that telling God all my secrets is what the Bible calls pouring out your heart to Him. I had no idea that pouring out your heart to God was also praying. I was so religious. I knew of

God but I did not really know Him. Thus, began my journey of discovering who God is and I am still learning.

I had a good night's rest and after taking the children to school, I took the bus to the hospital. Because they were expecting me, I did not have to wait long. I was ushered into a procedure room where I changed into hospital ware. The nurse scrubbed my abdomen in preparation for the test.

I almost fainted at the sight of the needle; it was even bigger than I imagined. So, I whispered "Jesus" throughout the procedure. Peace came. Then fear left and the pain disappeared.

The procedure took about twenty minutes. Soon after, I started having contractions I was transferred to a room in Labor and

Delivery Unit to be closely monitored and to receive an intravenous medication to stop the labor. I left the hospital a six that evening and was on time picking the kids up from aftercare. When we got home, I ordered pizza, helped the children with their bath, and thanked God that no one had homework. I staggered to bed and told the kids that I had a headache.

Pretending to be my nurses, they both climbed in bed with me. I was too tired to argue with them, so I slept.

CHAPTER 6

HOLDING ON TO THE PROMISE

I was actually home the next evening at six when Dr. K. called. He said, "I just wanted to tell you I got your result and everything is fine. Your baby does not have Down Syndrome or any other birth defects that we can see. Do you want to know the sex?" I said, "Yes." "It's a boy," he said. I replied, "Thank You, Jesus."

"All is well," continued Dr. K. "See you next week," and hung up.

Just like that, the storm was over. What I learned that day is that God is indeed good all the time. Even in difficult seasons, He is still good.

To say that I was happy about this news would be an understatement. I laughed and cried, all in the same breath. My children stared at me with big round eyes not knowing what to do. I hugged and kissed them and told them I had just gotten some good news, so they began jumping up and down celebrating with me. We had cookies and milk and watched a Power Ranger video. The children thanked God slept in their own beds that night.

Strangely enough, I had trouble sleeping that night. I was trying to come up with a strategy to announce my pregnancy to all my family and friends at the same time.

Ordinarily, I hated confrontation but in that particular case, I took my stand and I refused to budge. I did not know then that grace and mercy through the person of Jesus was working on my behalf the minute I accepted the second chance He gave me. Things started to change for me. People, even complete strangers began to give me stuff.

I got free meals, uniforms for clinical, bus passes and even money. I got a grant from the school, thanks to the Dean, Dr. Wines, who refused to let me quit because of finances. I had such a grace for memorization, that when I took a test I would remember the page even the paragraph where the answer was. The one thing that was stressing me, was finding an opportunity to make the announcement to all that I was almost seven months pregnant.

I truly dreaded that part. It was going to be everybody against me and the baby.

"O Lord," I prayed, "Help me." And He did.

That weekend, we visited my mom in Brooklyn, where she lived. The children were so excited. They talked nonstop but I was too preoccupied to hear what they were saying. While we were at the table eating dinner, my mom suddenly put her fork down and casually asked me, "When are you due?"

I had just taken a sip of my juice and it went down the wrong way. I started coughing and coughing which gave me some time to think. When I finally stopped coughing I answered "November 29," which was based on the baby's size. "How did you know," I asked her. Mom said, "You have been drinking milk, eating a plateful of vegetables without complaining and you are not relaxing your hair. We all know that you can only do lactose when you're pregnant and you only eat healthy when you're pregnant and you avoid chemicals especially in your hair." I finally looked at my husband. He kept on eating and did not say a word. I figured he did not want my mom to know that I did not tell him either.

I then told Greg and Ash who had stopped eating, "You guys are going to get a baby brother." They were ecstatic! They began to argue as to who was more responsible and who would babysit. With everything now out in the open, I breathed a sigh of relief and enjoyed my dinner. I knew that it was not over just yet. I was going to have to face the music once we got home.

As predicted, as soon as the door to our bedroom closed, my husband asked me, "So what happened?" I told him almost everything leaving out the Down Syndrome scare and the Amniocentesis. I concluded, "I know what you think, but I don't care, I am having this baby. Feel free to do whatever you deem necessary. The kids and I will be fine." As I drifted to sleep that night I thought since the secret was out maybe things would get back to normal now.

CHAPTER 7

HERE COMES THE PROMISE

There were no more surprises for the remainder of the pregnancy. I continued to use the cane for support and my knee continued to hurt especially after a long day. The kids and I spoke to the baby all the time. It was impossible to rest with them around. They took turns telling the baby their secrets.

I told them that they could pick their brother's name. My only specification was that the name ended with a "y." The first few names were awful. This caused them to go into fits of laughter. "Philly" as in Philly cheese steak, "Tommy and Jerry" for Tom and Jerry the cartoon, then Timothy, which was OK. But when they finally submitted Randy for approval. Their brother seemed to like it a lot, so it was our pick.

During that time, there was an uneasy truce at home. My husband and I avoided spending time alone. I hid behind a book most of the time on the pretext of studying.

The only cloud hanging over my head was that the school notified me that I could not miss more than three days of classes. If I did, I would have to repeat the quarter regardless of my grades. I prayed about it and gave it to God like everything else. I got a surprise baby shower from my friends and classmates. Once again God gave me favor and provided all that was needed for the baby. I received a car seat, bassinet, diapers, and lots of baby clothes and toys.

On Friday, November 18, I left school at 4 PM after taking my second final and took the express bus home. I picked up the children from aftercare and got Chinese takeout for dinner. By the time we finished dinner I was so drained, all I wanted was sleep. I propped myself on the sofa in the living room so I could keep an eye on the children.

I was awakened from a deep sleep by severe back pain. It took me a while for me to get up from the sofa. I checked on the kids who had also fallen asleep fully dressed. I gave them a sponge bath and put them in their pajamas before leaving their room. Since my back was getting worse, I began to time the cramps to see whether it was a false alarm.

Fifteen minutes later I decided that I indeed was in labor. I phoned my mother-in-law who lived a floor below us to come and stay with the children and paged the doctor and my husband from work. I then took a quick shower got dressed and waited for my husband to drive me to the hospital.

It was a short drive to the hospital and since I pre-registered I got to the Labor and Delivery unit in record time. I was examined by a Resident. My nurse started an intravenous line in my left arm and hooked me up to a fetal monitor. The labor was progressing slowly, but by 12 AM the next day, all pain stopped. I was told that I would probably be going home in the morning since I was only two and a half centimeters dilated.

My husband went home and I spent the night in the hospital. Dr. K. stopped by to see me at 11 AM. To his surprise he found me to be four and one-half centimeters dilated, so I could not go home. He ordered a Pitocin drip to accelerate the labor and went to see other patients.

My son Randy was born exactly an hour after the drip started while my husband went out to move his car to a different parking area. He had a huge curly afro and looked exactly like me. We bonded. He opened his eyes every time he heard my voice. We were fascinated with each other.

Seeing Randy trustingly put his head on my chest brought tears to my eyes. I thanked God profusely for His abundant grace and mercy. He truly showered me with His grace by giving me a miracle that I know I did not deserve.

CHAPTER 8

GOD IS GOOD ALL THE TIME

When God gave me this miracle twenty-four years ago, I did not know Him as a good Father because I did not have a good father. I knew nothing about His grace or His mercy, yet I encountered them both in the person of Jesus Christ. I have since that time gotten to know Him a lot better through His Holy Spirit. I found out the truth for myself, that God is good all the time.

We often say this at church but we don't really believe it. I had no idea that the God of the universe would listen to, much less answer my little one-line prayer, but He did. Because of His great love for me, He came down to my level and showered me with His love, grace, and mercy.

God gave Randy and I such favor, that I never lacked babysitters. In fact, he was such a charming baby that people volunteered to watch him while I stayed home to study. My last quarter at school was a breeze. I graduated with a 3.7-grade point average by the grace of God with my whole family in attendance including Randy!

I went on to successfully sit for my state board exam and officially became a Registered Nurse. The first thing I did was to return to Social Services and cancel the benefits that I had been receiving. My case worker was very touched. But God was not done with us yet. I applied for a job along with two hundred other applicants and got it. While my marriage seemed to be at a standstill, Randy, on the other hand, was growing by leaps and bounds. He copied everything his siblings did.

By age two he spoke clearly using full sentences. And even though he was a quiet child, he did not allow himself to be bullied-something his siblings quickly learned. He did well in kindergarten and was the proverbial social butterfly.

In first grade, Randy's teacher reported that he always looked bored, and did not pay attention in class, so she questioned whether or not he had a learning disability. The school tested him and it turned out that he read at the third-grade level and was quickly placed in a gifted program, which lasted until high school.

God got the last laugh! My marriage ended in 2001 and the children and I relocated to Atlanta.

Randy started Junior High in Georgia and was still in a gifted program. The summer before his freshman year in high school, he stopped eating junk food and ran a few miles every day. He always had lots of friends from different ethnic backgrounds, but the girls took notice when he showed up in school lean, buff and fashion conscious.

By his sophomore year, Randy had a group of friends that I did not really care for. I seemed to be the only parent of the group with rules. We did not really have arguments but I would say one thing to which Randy agreed, knowing that he was going to do the opposite.

I learned to contend for my miracle through prayer, fasting and declaring the word of God over all of my children. I cover them daily with the blood of Jesus and declare that angels surround them and will snatch them out of danger in a minute and in the blink of an eye. Over and over again I have seen them miraculously saved from accidents and other dangerous situations.

Randy had a group of friends that I had some reservations about. You see, he was the lone Black kid in their midst. They were involved in all kinds of mischiefs and I was greatly concerned. He quit the gifted program so he could hang out with them. I only found this out at the end of his junior year of high school.

The school allowed Randy to leave without my signature. I began to pray in earnest that God would remove these friends from Randy's life. There is no other way to say it, The Lord rebuked me. He called my prayer a selfish prayer and told me to pray for the other kids, in the same way, I prayed for my children.

I began to bless the chairs they sat on; the bottled water that they drank from as a point of contact for God to touch them. I had a strong suspicion they were drinking alcohol, though I never actually caught them. So, I prayed earnestly that they would encounter angels on my property and change their mind about God.

Randy graduated from High School in 2012 at age seventeen. He enrolled the following Fall at Georgia Southern University, four hours away from where we lived. After his freshman year, Randy asked for a semester off. His dad and I agreed. One semester became two until he finally told me that college was not for him. I was devastated. So I bombarded heaven with prayer and intercession on his behalf. The Lord's answer, "Don't worry I got him."

I gave my children back to God and relinquished all my rights. When the enemy would come to tell me what he had planned for them, I would simply redirect him to God their Father. I am only a temporary guardian, and as such, I enjoy peace because of my absolute trust in God.

That trust came in handy one evening when Randy burst into my bedroom followed by two Fayetteville police officers with guns drawn. Their explanation did not make any sense. They saw three white teenagers and one black going toward the back of a house and thought that there was a home invasion. I had planned to meet with some friends that evening and canceled out of the blue without knowing why.

The enemy attempted the same attack one other time while I was away on a travel assignment. A young man came over my house to fight with one of Randy's friends with a knife. He was overpowered by the group. When he got to his car, he called the police. The same two trigger happy cops came to my house once again. Even though I was not there, the blood of Jesus and the word of God I had declared over my children and my house did not fail.

I know that God loves my children more than I do and that He has great plans for them, therefore my eyes are fixed on Him and not on what I see with my natural eyes. I make it a practice to declare from the word of God the opposite of what I see with my natural eyes.

Randy went through a rebellious stage where he not only quit college, he refused to get a job. Through it all, I stood on the word of God. He dyed his hair half blond and half black for a time. When I went before God to complain, He gave me a dream. I saw Randy well dressed in a tuxedo and nice haircut. I woke up with the peace of God on my heart and mind and never mentioned his hair again.

When he stopped attending church, questioning the word of God, The Lord told me to keep praying not to give up. In October of 2017, Randy had a dream warning him to make a choice. He rededicated his life to God with me over the phone.

You see, God has no grandchildren, only children. We each have to experience his goodness for ourselves regardless of other people's testimonies. Like a natural father, God will teach them His ways, discipline them and reward them. My prayer was that Randy would know his success in life was because of the grace of God.

Randy's gifts and talents are for God's purpose through him on earth. I continue to stand in the gap for my children to see them fulfill their destinies and bring glory to God. I continue to see things with my eyes of faith and declare the word of God over them daily, including these affirmations:

- My children are saved and are on fire for God. (Acts 16:31)

- My children are disciples of Christ. (Matthew 19:14)(Isaiah 54:13)

- My children know their God and they are strong and will do great exploits for Him. Daniel 11:32b)

- Their days will not be cut short. They will fulfill all their allotted days on earth. (Psalms 139:16)(Psalms 118:17)

- Their lives will glorify God. (Colossians 3:23)

Fast forward to 2018:

Randy is now twenty-four years old. He is a creative young man with a passion for skateboarding and music. In addition to making his own beats, he works in a recording studio where he helps others to make their dreams come true. He is living the prophetic word spoken over his life. He is learning to trust God in every area of his life while seeking a closer relationship with Him.

CHAPTER 9

COME MEET GRACE AND MERCY

When I made that terrible decision twenty-four years ago, I did not know to run to God because of the nature of the sin, but Grace and Mercy found me. In my darkest hour, hopelessly depressed and alone, I encountered Grace and Mercy in the person of Jesus Christ.

Although I was a baby in the faith, He got down to my level and ministered to my heart. He gave me His strength when I could not stand on my own. He gave me grace and favor with others around me. He gave me great grace to believe that my son would be fine when everything else was pointing to the contrary.

I was so hurt and broken inside, but he healed me and made me whole again. Today, you, too, can have an encounter with Jesus. Guilt and condemnation are not of God. If you had one abortion or several, the only way you can silence the accuser is to repent. Get on your knees right now and ask God to forgive you. Ask Him to cleanse you, and to heal your breaches.

The Bible states in Hebrews 10:17 that once you confess your sins, that God remembers them no more. Then we find in Psalms 103:12, "As far as the East is from the

West, so far He removed our transgressions from us."

To give your life to Jesus or recommit to a fresh new start with Him, pray this prayer with all your heart:

"Father God, I believe in my heart you sent your son, Jesus, to die on the cross in my place. He rose again on the third day. Lord Jesus, come into my heart. Save me. Forgive my sins. Cleanse me with your precious blood. Fill me with your Holy Spirit. Thank you, Lord, for saving me." Just like that, your past no longer exists. You are now a new creature.

Join a Holy Spirit-filled, Bible-believing church. Get baptized in water and in The Holy Spirit. Keep renewing your mind in the word of God daily.

The Christian disciplines of prayer and fasting will help you to grow spiritually. Be available so that God can use you in his end-time global harvest. Most importantly, use your faith! The Father has given us great grace to imitate Christ and to trust in Him.

May you be filled to overflowing from this day onward with the peace of God that passes all understanding, giving all glory and praise to Jesus.

Amen.

ABOUT THE AUTHOR
YVES-MARIE GALETTE

Yves-Marie Galette was born in Port-au-Prince Haiti. She became orphan at the age of 5. She was raised by her maternal grandmother and her maternal aunt who later became her adoptive mother. She survived both physical abuse and sexual molestation. As a result of the pain and loss she endured in her childhood, she has a heart for orphans, the lost and broken. Her desire is for them to experience and to be transformed by the love of God.

To Contact Yves-Marie Galette about her future works or ministry please visit her Blog Page, *For the Sake of Love*, at the following address:

https://forthesakeoflove.net/

Made in the USA
Coppell, TX
08 February 2023